SCHOLASTIC

Traits Writing™

Writing Journal

Credits appear on page 96, which constitutes an extension of this copyright page.

Copyright © 2011 by Scholastic Inc.

All rights reserved.   Published by Scholastic Inc.   Printed in the U.S.A.

ISBN-13: 978-0-545-35806-4

ISBN-10: 0-545-35806-X

SCHOLASTIC, TRAITS WRITING, and associated logos are trademarks and/or registered trademarks of Scholastic Inc.

Other company names, brand names, and product names are the property and/or trademarks of their respective owners. Scholastic does not endorse any product or business entity mentioned herein.

11 12 13 14 15   40   20 19 18

 Text pages printed on 10% PCW recycled paper.

Welcome!

Ready to write? Let's go!

Draw a picture of yourself. Then write your name.

Contents

Getting Started

She caught the person

MY LUCKY CAT

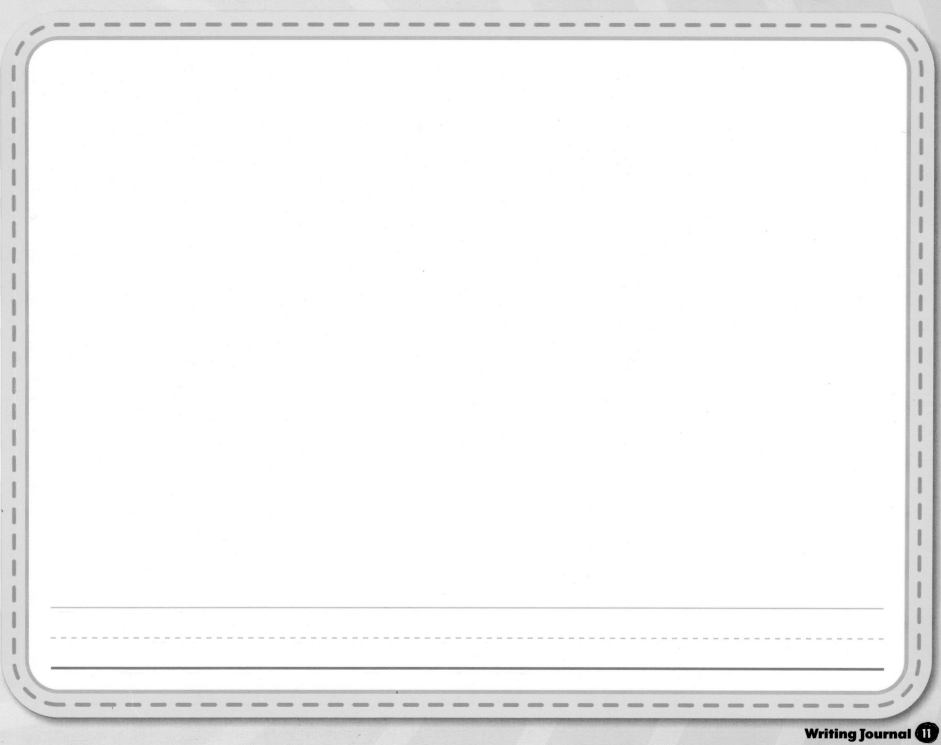

Ideas

Ideas

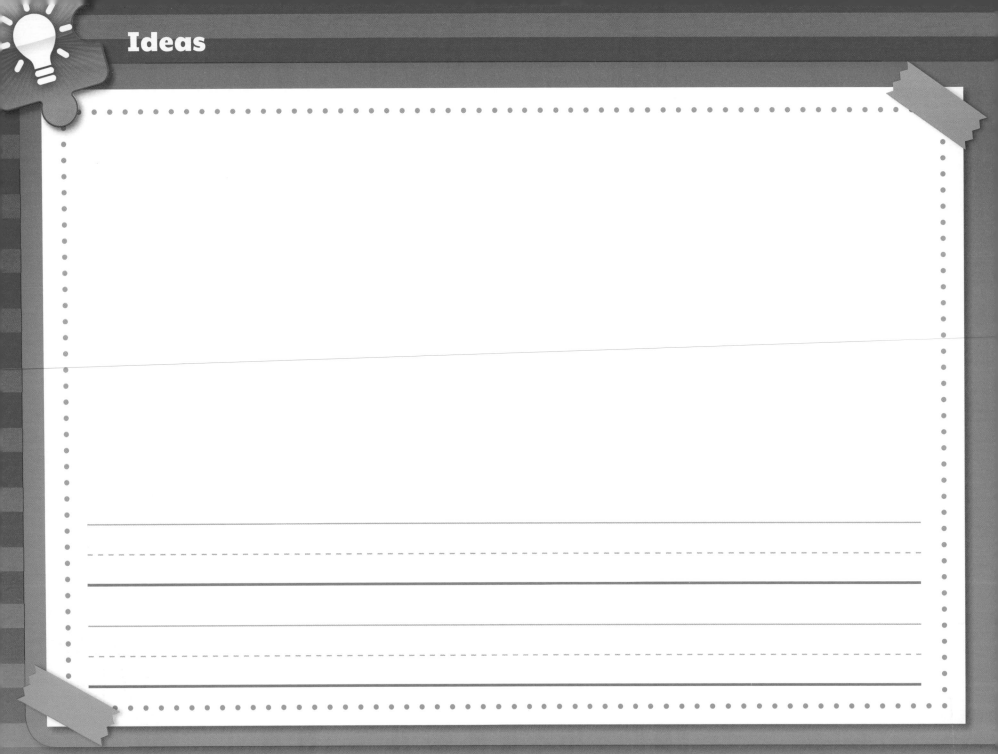

Organization

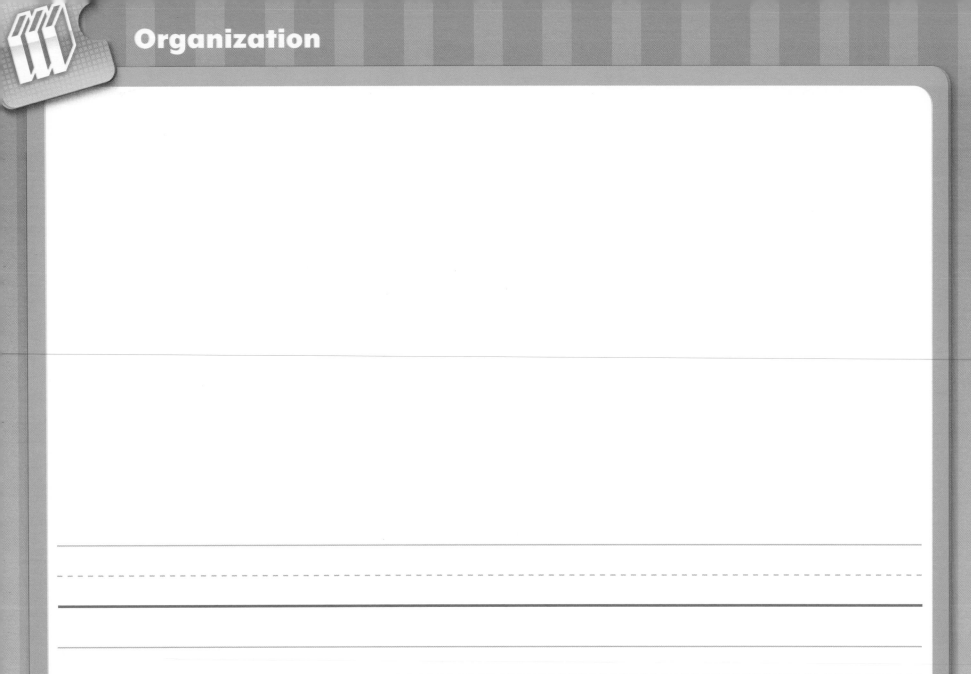

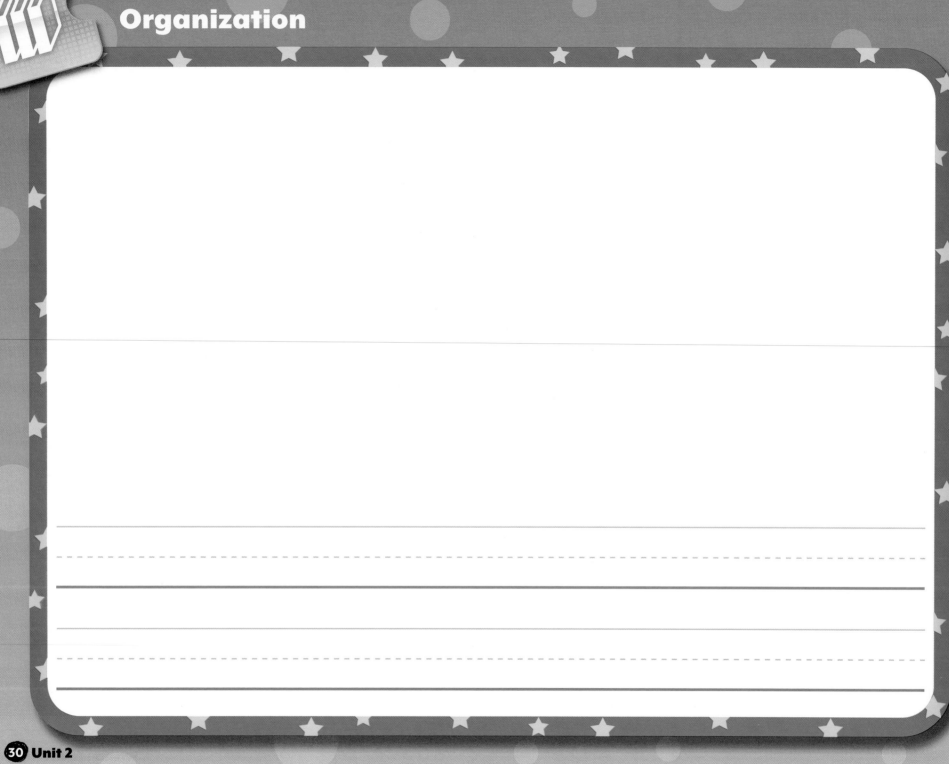

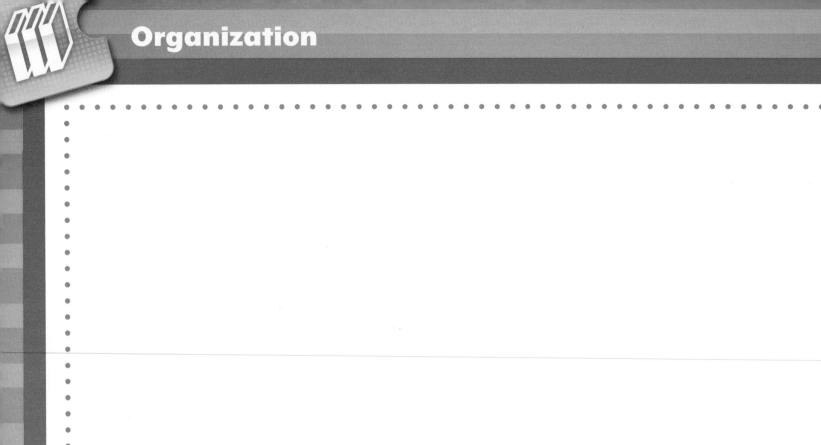

Organization

Voice

Voice

37

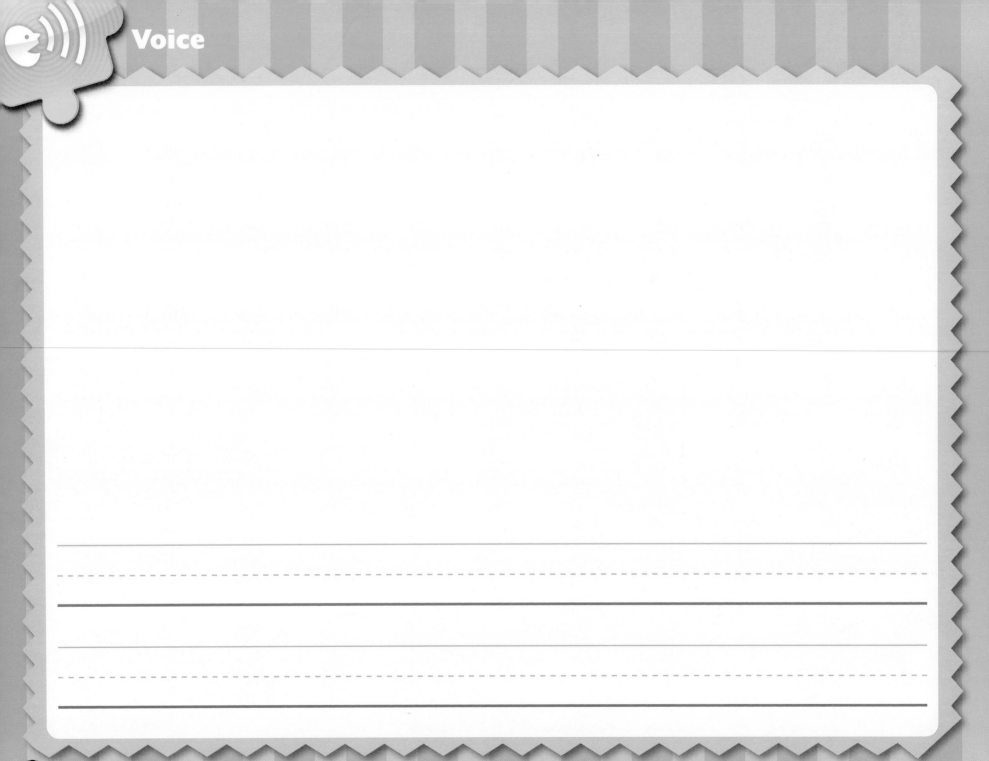

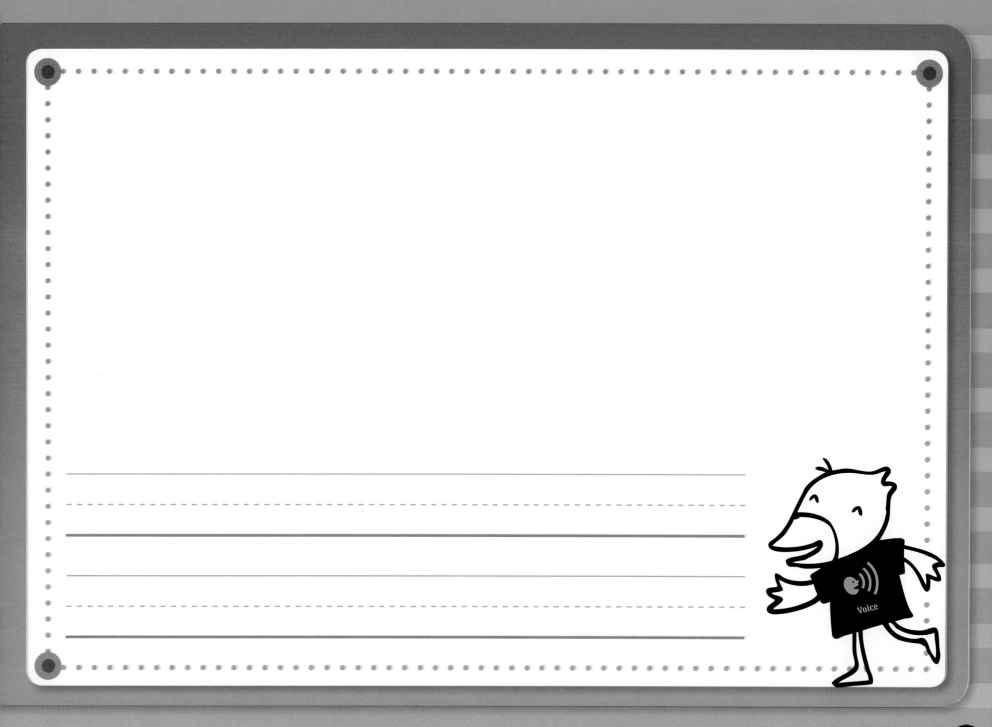

Word Choice

Word Choice

Word Choice

Sentence Fluency

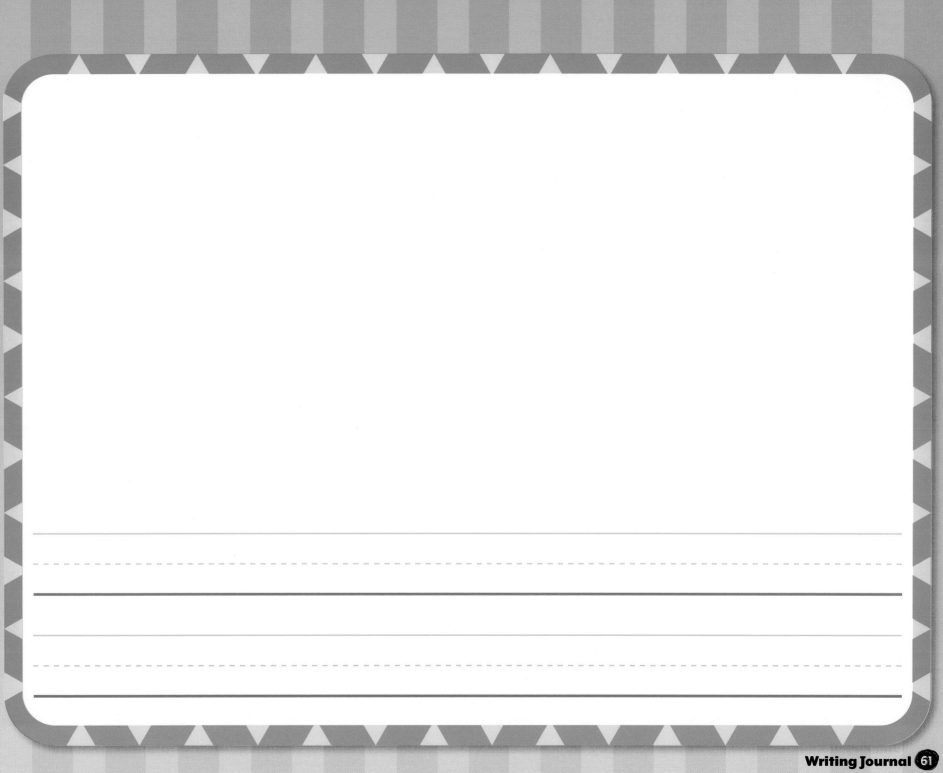

All Traits

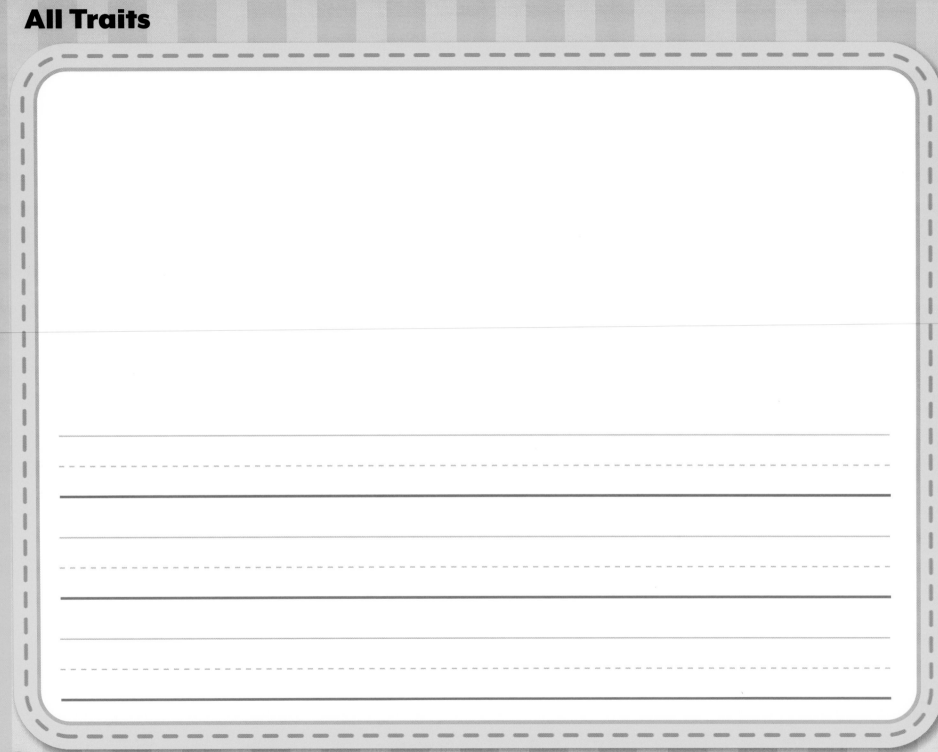

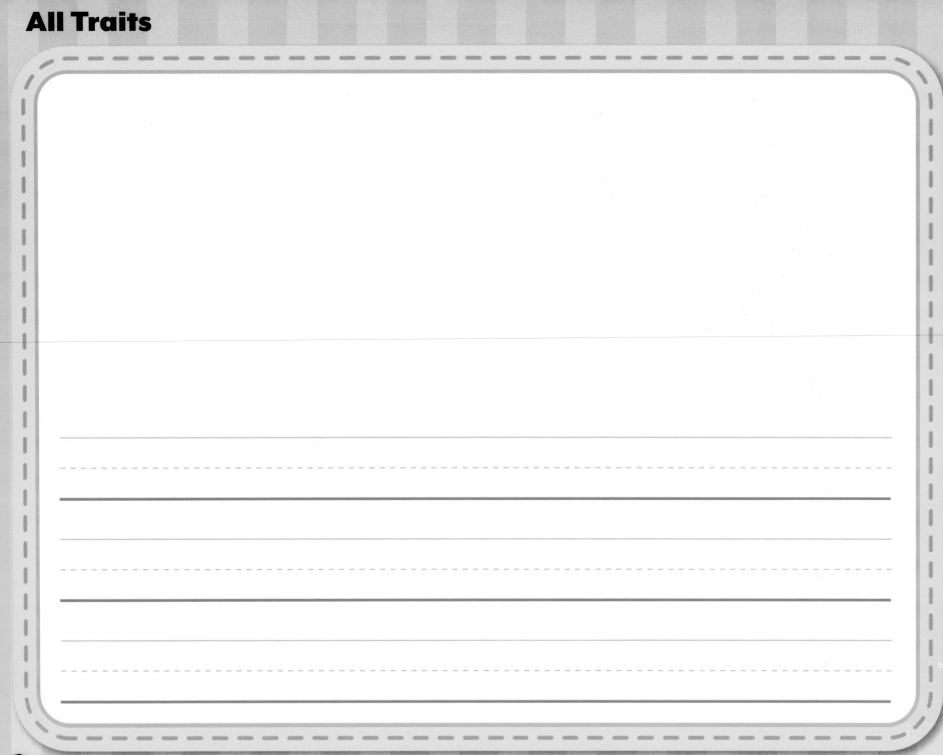

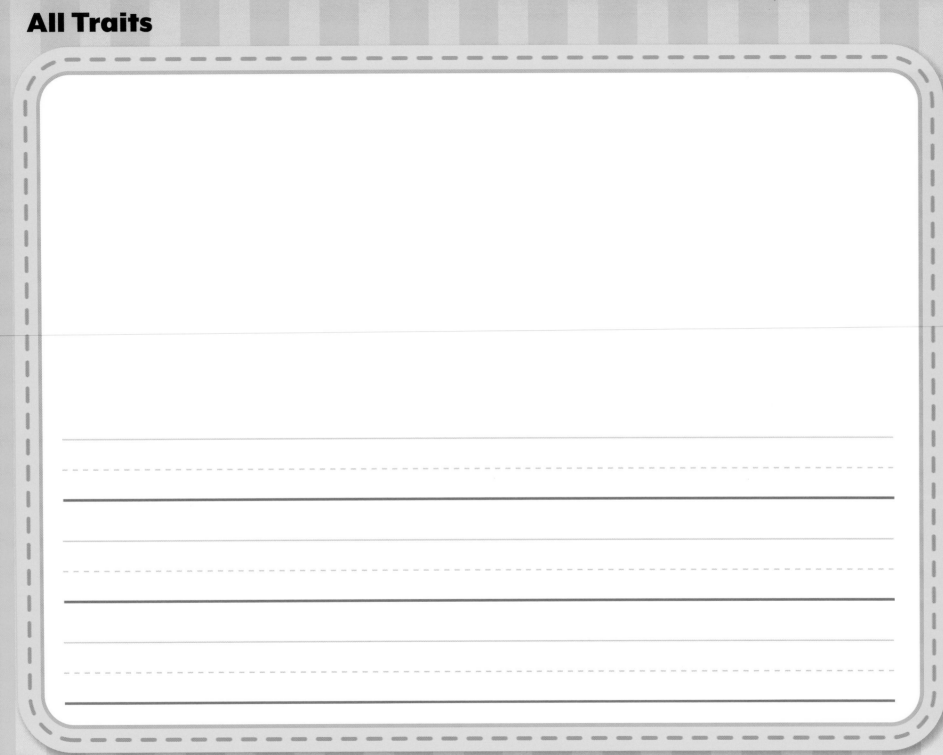

All Traits

My Spelling Words

Conventions

My Spelling Words

My Spelling Words

Conventions

My Spelling Words

My Spelling Words

My Spelling Words

My Spelling Words

Handwriting

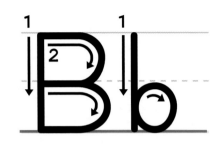

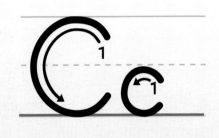 

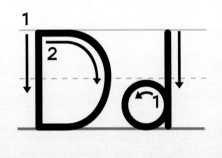

 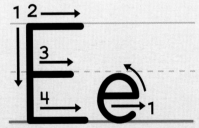

 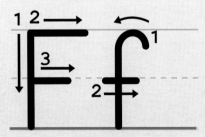

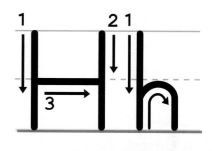

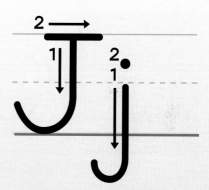

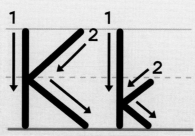

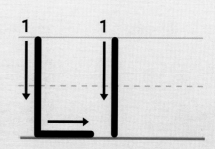

Handwriting

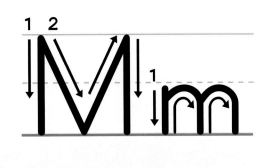

Mm

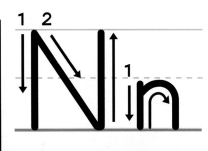

Nn

Oo

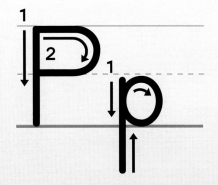

Pp

Qq

Rr

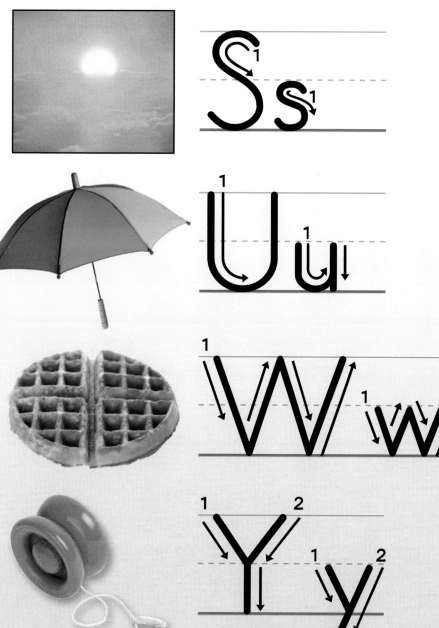

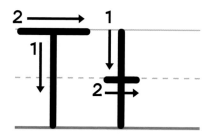

Ss Tt

Uu Vv

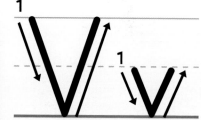

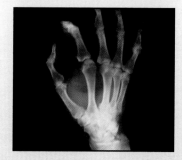

Ww Xx

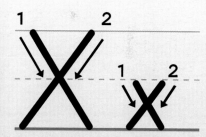

Yy

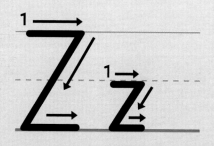

Zz

Letter to Next Year's Teacher

Dear Teacher,

Your new student,

_____
(your name)

Ideas

I have a topic, and I know a lot about it.

Just Starting

On My Way

I've Got It!

Organization

I put my ideas in an order that makes sense.

Just Starting

On My Way

I've Got It!

Voice

I made sure my writing sounds like me.

Just Starting

On My Way

I've Got It!

Word Choice

I picked colorful, just-right words.

Just Starting

On My Way

I've Got It!

Sentence Fluency

I wrote sentences that sound great.

Just Starting

On My Way

I've Got It!

Conventions

I cleaned up my writing for my reader.

Just Starting

On My Way

I've Got It!

Presentation

I dressed up my writing so it's ready to share.

Just Starting

On My Way

I've Got It!

Credits